A first guide to

◆

Greece

By Kath Davies

A ZOË BOOK

A *ZOË BOOK*

© 2000 Zoë Books Limited

Devised and produced by
Zoë Books Limited
15 Worthy Lane
Winchester
Hampshire SO23 7AB
England

First published in Great Britain in 2000 by
Zoë Books Limited
15 Worthy Lane
Winchester
Hampshire SO23 7AB

A record of the CIP data is available from the British Library.

ISBN 1 874488 97 5

Printed in Hong Kong by Midas Printing Ltd.
Design: Sterling Associates
Map: Sterling Associates
Picture research: Bob Davidson
Production: Grahame Griffiths

Photographic acknowledgments

The publishers wish to acknowledge, with thanks, the following photographic sources:

Cover: Impact Photos/Christopher Bluntzer; Title page & 5l: Zefa; 5r The Hutchison Library/ Ron Giling; 6 Lesley & Roy Adkins Picture Library; 7l TRIP/M Dubin; 7r TRIP/G Zefeiropoulos; 8 DDA Photo Library/I.Z. Dawson; 9l TRIP/M Dubin; 9r NHPADaniel Heuclin; 10 TRIP/P Terry; 11l The Hutchison Library/Bernard Régent; 11r Lesley & Roy Adkins Picture Library; 12 The Hutchison Library/Andrew Hill; 13l Zefa; 13r Robert Harding Picture Library/David Beatty; 14 Impact Photos/Mark Henley; 15l DDA Photo Library/ I.Z.Dawson; 15r The Hutchison Library/Andrew Hill; 16 Zefa; 17l The Hutchison Library/Bernard Régent; 17r TRIP/G Gunnarsson; 18 The Hutchison Library/John Egan; 19l Impact Photos/ Caroline Penn; 19r The Hutchison Library/John Egan; 20 Impact Photos/Mark Henley; 21l The Hutchison Library/Robert Aberman; 21r Impact Photos/ Alex Dufort; 22 e.t.archive; 23l Lesley & Roy Adkins Picture Library; 23r The Hutchison Library/John Egan; 24 Lesley & Roy Adkins Picture Library; 25l DDA Photo Library/ I.Z.Dawson; 25r e.t.archive/National Archaelogical Museum, Naples; 26 e.t.archive; 27l Lesley & Roy Adkins Picture Library; 27r e.t.archive/The Parker Gallery; 28 e.t.archive; 29l AKG/London; 29r The Hutchison Library/Nancy Durrell McKenna.

The publishers have made every effort to trace the copyright holders, but if they have inadvertently overlooked any, they will be pleased to make the necessary arrangement at the first opportunity.

Cover: *The Acropolis, above the modern city of Athens*

Title page: *Pinnacles of rock at Metéora*

Contents

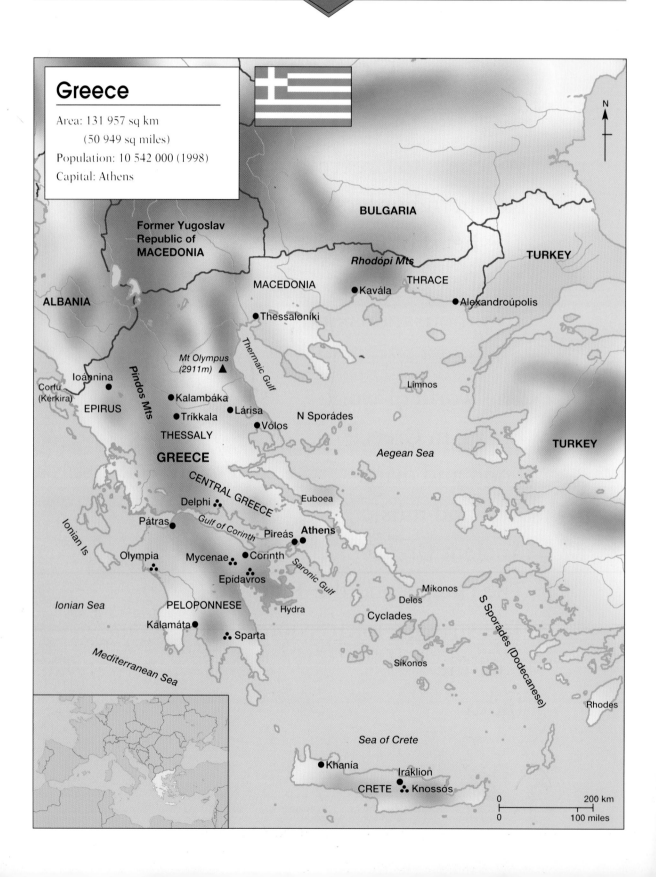

Greece

Area: 131 957 sq km
     (50 949 sq miles)
Population: 10 542 000 (1998)
Capital: Athens

N

Former Yugoslav
Republic of
MACEDONIA

BULGARIA

Rhodópi Mts

TURKEY

MACEDONIA

THRACE

●Kavála

●Alexandroúpolis

ALBANIA

Thessaloníki

*Mt Olympus
(2911m)* ▲

Thermaic Gulf

●Ioánnina

Corfu
(Kérkira)

Pindos Mts

EPIRUS

●Kalambáka

●Láarisa

●Trikkala

●Vólos

THESSALY

Limnos

N Sporádes

Aegean Sea

TURKEY

GREECE

CENTRAL GREECE

Euboea

Delphi

Ionian Is

Pátras●

Gulf of Corinth

Pireás

Athens

Olympia

Mycenae

●Corinth

Saronic Gulf

Epídavros

Ionian Sea

PELOPONNESE

Hydra

Míkonos

Delos

Cyclades

S Sporádes (Dodecanese)

Kalamáta●

Sparta

Mediterranean Sea

Síkonos

Rhodes

Sea of Crete

●Khanía

Iráklion

CRETE ●Knossós

0   200 km
0   100 miles

Welcome to Greece

Welcome to Greece! *Kalós éelthate*! Greece is a small country on the Mediterranean Sea. There are thousands of small islands around its coast.

Most of the land in Greece is mountainous. Farmers grow crops on the plains and the high, flat land. The summers are hot and dry. Winters are usually mild, but there is snow in the north. There are often earthquakes.

▼ A village on the island of Síkinos

▲ Selling newspapers in Athens

The Greek countryside has small villages and groves of olive trees. Some village churches are hundreds of years old. There are older ruined temples, too.

The ancient Greeks lived about 2500 years ago. They were soldiers, sailors and traders. The Greeks' way of ruling the country was copied by other European countries.

There are two forms of the Greek language. One form is used in the law courts and the Greek church. The other form is used for every day. The Greek alphabet dates back to ancient times.

Northern borders

In the northern region of Macedonia, farmers grow wheat and tobacco. They keep sheep and goats in the mountains. Macedonia was a kingdom about 2400 years ago. Today, this name also belongs to a nearby country.

Nearly half a million people live in Thessaloníki. It is a busy seaport. Factories here have polluted the sea in the Thermaic Gulf. There are new blocks of flats and offices in the city, and old city walls. Some of the churches are more than 1000 years old. They are decorated with pictures called mosaics.

To the south of Thessaloníki three fingers of land stretch south into the Aegean Sea.

▼ Fishing boats in the northern port of Kavála

▲ Orthodox monks on Mount Athos

Many holiday-makers enjoy the pine woods and sandy beaches here.

Roads to the east

Many kinds of people live in Thrace. There are Moslems who speak Turkish, and Christians who speak Greek. Farmers grow cotton and tobacco here. The main port is Alexandroúpolis.

In the north are the Rhodópi mountains, and to the east is the Turkish border.

Holy mountain

Some Christian churches are called the Orthodox churches. Orthodox priests have beards and wear tall black hats.

The Greek for Mount Athos means 'holy mountain'. Mount Athos has twenty monasteries on it. They were set up about 1000 years ago. The monks who live there belong to the Greek Orthodox Church. They look after the whole area.

▼ Hills of salt at Thessaloníki

The heart of Greece

To the south of Macedonia is Thessaly, where farmers grow wheat, fruit and olives. The main towns here are Tríkkala, Lárisa and the busy port of Vólos.

Mount Olympus lies in the north. It is 2917 metres (9551 feet) high. The summit is snow-capped for most of the year. Wild flowers and herbs grow there in summer. The ancient Greeks thought that the gods and goddesses lived there.

There are strange rock shapes at Metéora, near Kalambáka. Hundreds of years ago, people built monasteries on top of these pointed rocks.

▼ The ruined temple of Apollo at Delphi

▲ Walkers on Mount Olympus.

Temples and vineyards

There are vineyards and olive groves in central Greece.

Delphi is on the slopes of Mount Parnassus. There was a temple here to Apollo, the god of light. In ancient times, people came to hear a priestess, called the oracle, chant messages about the future.

The far west

Sheep and goats graze in the region of Epirus. The chief city is Ionánnina on the shores of Lake Pamvótis.

Wildlife

Snakes, vultures, lizards and geckos live in Greece. There are a few wolves, wild boar and brown bear in the mountains. Now, forests have been cut down and many wild animals are in danger.

A story tells how an ancient Greek writer, Aschylus, was killed when an eagle dropped a tortoise on his head! Greece still has eagles and tortoises.

▼ Hermann's tortoise

The Peloponnese

This is the name of a peninsula in southern Greece. In the centre and south, there are mountains with valleys and spectacular gorges. The biggest city is Kalamata, famous for exporting olives.

The Corinth Canal is more than 6 kilometres (6 miles) long. It cuts through sheer rock across a narrow strip of land called the Isthmus of Corinth. The canal was built in 1893 to join the Ionian and Aegean seas. Ships enter Greece through the port of Pátras at the western end of the Gulf of Corinth.

▼ Ancient buildings at Mistrás, near Sparta in the Peloponnese

▲ The Corinth Canal

A motorway runs along the north coast through Corinth and on to Athens.

Ancient sites

Visitors come to see the ancient sites such as the city of Corinth. It was one of the grandest cities in the world in ancient Greek and Roman times. At Mycenae there is a fortress which is 4000 years old.

Sparta was a powerful state about 2500 years ago. Warriors there were tough and war-like. Epídavros was a centre of healing. Its famous theatre is still used.

The Olympic Games

The first Olympic games were probably held at Olympia in about 1370BCE (Before the Christian Era). The games included long jump, javelin and discus, throwing, running races, wrestling and chariot racing.

▼ The ancient Greeks decorated pottery with pictures. This picture shows a discus thrower.

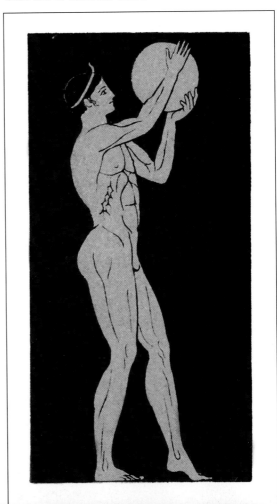

Two thousand islands

Greece is a mountainous country. It was easier for the ancient Greeks to travel by sea than by land. Today, fishing boats, ferries and cruise ships use the sea routes around Greece.

There are about 2000 Greek islands. Most of them have sandy beaches. There are old buildings, churches and castles on these islands. The islanders work at fishing and farming, with some mining and quarrying.

Tourism has brought changes to the islands, and many people now work in hotels and restaurants.

▼ A harbour on the island of Hydra

▲ A windmill on Míkonos

From sea to sea

The Ionian islands are just off the west coast of Greece. Corfu is the largest Ionian island. It is very popular with tourists. Venice ruled Corfu from 1386 until 1797.

The Cyclades are islands in the Aegean Sea. Delos was a holy island, and has many ruined temples. Míkonos is famous for windmills and narrow, whitewashed streets.

The Sporadés islands stretch from the northwest in the Aegean Sea to the southeast, near the coast of Turkey. Rhodes is the largest of the Sporadés islands. It was a base for the Knights of St John. They fought against the Moslems in the holy wars called the Crusades.

Crete

Crete is Greece's largest island. It has high mountains and deep caves and gorges. Farmers keep sheep and goats, and grow potatoes, olives, and grapes for wine-making.

The two main cities are Iráklion and Khánia. There are many tourist towns around the coast. Crete has its own customs and dress, and its own form of the Greek language.

▼ People wearing traditional dress

Athens

There is a hill called the Acropolis in the city of Athens. People have lived there for more than 7000 years. The temple on the hill, the Parthenon, was built more than 1500 years ago. A huge statue of the city's goddess, Athena, once stood there.

Greek and Roman ruins can be seen in Athens. Traffic pollutes the air and wears away the stones, so the city is banning cars from its centre. Today, Athens has busy shops, offices and markets. People sell newspapers, sweets and snacks on the street.

▼ The city of Athens and the Acropolis

What to see

Athens is full of things to see. The views from the Acropolis are wonderful. There are huge temples and a gateway here.

At the foot of the Acropolis is the Plaka. This area has many small lanes full of shops, restaurants and museums.

There are beautiful works of art from ancient times, such as pottery and gold from Mycenae, in the National Archaeological Museum.

▼ A street in the Plaka

▲ A passenger ship at Pireás

The port of Pireás

Pireás is the port of Athens. There are shipbuilding yards, oil refineries and factories here. The harbour is full of tankers, ferries and passenger ships. People take ferries to the islands from Pireás.

Ships from Pireás travel to other Mediterranean ports such as Alexandria in Egypt.

The world of work

Greece has a dry climate, and there is not much good farmland. The country has been very poor. Many people went to live and work in other countries, such as the United States of America (USA), Germany or Australia.

▲ Holiday-makers in northern Greece

Since 1981, Greece has been part of the European Union (EU). There are now more factories and industries such as oil refining and textile making. Tourists come to Greece from all over the world. They enjoy the sunny weather, warm seas and sandy beaches. They also visit the villages and the ancient sites.

▲ A sponge-seller in Athens

Work in tourism

Tourism has brought all types of jobs to Greece. Many people are travel guides and drivers. Others work in hotels and restaurants as waiters and cooks.

People need places to stay. Some bring their boats with them. New holiday flats have been built, and marinas for boats. Some people work in banks, shops or offices.

Farming and fishing

More than a quarter of Greek people work in farming and fishing. They keep sheep and goats on the poorer land, and make cheese and yoghurt from the milk. On richer land, farmers grow crops such as lemons, water melons, maize, wheat, sunflowers and tomatoes. Greek fishing boats bring in tuna, mullet, squid and octopus.

Olives have been an important crop in Greece for thousands of years.

▼ Harvesting olives on Crete

Living in Greece

Life is busy in towns and cities. There are offices, shops and flats, and cinemas and theatres to visit. There is a lot of noisy traffic. In the countryside, there is not so much traffic. Life in the villages is quieter.

However, the climate affects everyone in Greece. It is hard to work when it is very hot. People work in the morning and evening, when it is cooler.

In cities and in villages, shops open late. People enjoy walking around, or sitting in the open air to talk with friends. They often talk about politics.

▼ People talk with friends and family at a village café.

Greek government

More than 2500 years ago, the people of Athens decided on a new way of governing. Instead of a king or an emperor, the people chose their own leaders. This type of government is called democracy. Many other countries have followed Greece and are now democracies.

Religion

Many Greek people belong to the Christian Orthodox Church.

▼ Priests lead an Easter procession

The most important festival of the Christian year is Easter. People usually spend Easter with their families. Children usually have a saint's name. They may have a party on that saint's 'name day', instead of on their own birthday.

Moving around

There are buses and taxis in towns, and airports in some cities. Motorways and railways link Athens with other towns. Smaller roads wind through the countryside.

People travel by bus or by donkey in the countryside. Boats sail from island to island and to the mainland.

▼ Donkeys on the island of Límnos

Food and drink

In Greece, people like to eat out of doors. Breakfast is not an important meal. Many people just drink coffee. Shops and offices close at about 2pm, and lunch is served between 2 and 3 o'clock. After work in the evening, people eat dinner between 9 and 11pm.

There are many different types of place to eat out. Tourists enjoy the town restaurants and bars, called *tavernas*. In villages there is usually a coffee house called a *cafenió*. Street markets sell fresh fruit and vegetables, and some stalls sell cheese or spinach pies. Bakeries sell bread and cakes as well as the traditional Greek sweet foods including the sticky *baklavá*.

▼ Cafés in Athens on a Sunday morning

▲ A fruit and vegetable stall

Greek meals

A Greek meal may start with a paste made from chickpeas, called *houmous*. Other favourites are fish-roe paste called *taramasaláta*, or cucumber with yoghurt and garlic, called *tsatzíki*.

Special Greek salads are made from tomatoes, olives and soft cheese called *fétta*. Main dishes include baked mince (*moussáka*), chicken or lamb stew with beans (*stifhádo*), and stuffed vine leaves (*dolmádes*). There are lots of fried fish and seafood such as squid or octopus.

Greek food such as kebabs and pitta bread are now popular around the world.

Many people enjoy Greek wines. The white wine called *retsína*, and a strong spirit called *oúzo*, are very popular. Coffee is strong and sweet. It is served in tiny cups.

▼ Greek lunch out of doors

Arts and music

People have admired the arts and crafts of ancient Greece for hundreds of years. There are beautiful wall paintings at Knossós on Crete, gold objects from Mycenae and wonderful statues and temples in Athens. Builders and craft workers in many countries have copied the Greek styles of buildings, pottery and sculpture.

About 2800 years ago, the poet Homer wrote poems about warriors, gods and goddesses. Sophocles and Euripides wrote plays around that time which are still performed today. Sometimes the ancient stone theatres are used. The plays are put on in the open air.

▼ A picture of Christ in the Byzantine style

▲ The ancient theatre at Epídavros

Holy pictures

About 800 years ago, the city of Byzantium (modern Istanbul) was a centre for the Christian religion.

Greek artists and monks made mosaics. They decorated the churches with them. They also painted pictures of saints, called icons, and decorated them with gold and jewels.

Writers and actors

Well-known Greek poets today include CP Cavafy and George Seferis. The novelist Nikos Kazantzakis wrote *Zorba the Greek*, which was filmed in 1965. The actress Melina Mercouri starred in this film.

Folk dance and music

Folk music is very popular in Greece. Each region of Greece has its own type of dance and music. Musicians may play a stringed instrument called a *bouzoúki*, or a small harp called a *sandoúri*. The harp is played with hammers. The violin and the bagpipes are played, too.

▼ Dancing on the island of Límnos

Ancient Greece

The first civilization in Greece is called Minoan. About 4500 years ago, the palace at Knossós on Crete was built for the ruler, called Minos. The wall paintings there tell us about life at court at that time. The Minoans made beautiful pottery, cloth and metalwork. They traded as far west as the British Isles.

A huge volcanic eruption destroyed the northern coast of Crete about 3500 years ago, and power passed to the rulers of states on the Greek mainland. The kings of Mycenae became very powerful.

▼ This wall painting from Knossós shows a Minoan priest-king.

▲ A sculpture of a chariot driver

The power of Greece

In ancient times, Greece was a collection of city-states. Each city, such as Athens, Sparta and Corinth, ruled the area around it. States often fought each other, but they fought together against other peoples such as the Celts and the Persians. About 2400 years ago, these states were very powerful. It was called a golden age.

Some Greeks sailed to countries such as modern Turkey, Italy, France, Spain and northern Africa. They settled there, and set up colonies.

Alexander the Great

In 338BCE, King Philip II of Macedonia defeated the other Greek states. After he was assassinated, his son, Alexander, ruled.

Alexander was a famous fighter. He was called Alexander the Great because he conquered many lands, including Persia and Egypt. His empire stretched all the way to northern India.

▼ This mosaic shows Alexander the Great in battle.

The Greeks and the Turks

About 2000 years ago, the Greek states became part of the Roman empire. The Roman emperor, Constantine, founded a new capital city at the Greek colony of Byzantium. He gave it his own name, Constantinople. It is called Istanbul today.

The city was the centre of a new empire which stretched around the Mediterranean Sea. It had Roman laws and customs,

▼ The Empress Theodora is in the middle of this mosaic picture.

▲ A small Byzantine monastery at Mistrás

the Greek language and the Christian religion. The empire was most powerful in the time of the empress Theodora and the law-maker Justinian. It grew weaker after the Crusaders attacked it in the Middle Ages.

Greece under the Turks

In 1387CE the Ottoman Turks began to attack Greece, and in 50 years they had destroyed the Byzantine empire. The Turks ruled from Constantinople.

The Greeks kept their own language and religion, but they paid taxes to the Turkish rulers.

The Greeks fight back

Many Greeks wanted freedom from Turkish rule. The Turks had made Greeks into slaves, and murdered thousands of people. There were rebellions in many parts of Greece between 1821 and 1827.

Western countries helped the Greeks to win their freedom.

They defeated the Turks in the sea battle at Navarino in 1827. In 1830, an international agreement recognised Greece as an independent nation.

▼ The Battle of Navarino

The struggle for freedom

The new Greek state had no king or queen. The people chose their own rulers. This type of state is called a republic. When the first president, Ioannis Capodistrias, tried to rule alone, as a dictator, he was assassinated. Some members of the European royal families then ruled, but they were not popular.

During this time, Greece fought against Turkey and Bulgaria over land. It joined Britain and the Allies in the First World War (1914-1918). After the war, Greece fought Turkey again, but was defeated.

▼ Greece, Turkey and Bulgaria all wanted to control Adrianople. Today it is in Turkey.

▲ Germans at Delphi in the Second World War

Governments

During the Second World War (1939-1945), the Germans invaded Greece. The country was freed by Allies, Greek royalist troops and Communist freedom-fighters called the *andartes*.

From 1944 until 1949 there was civil war in Greece. The Allies and the royalists fought the Communists.

Greece became a monarchy again in 1949, but in 1967, army officers seized power. The King was forced to leave the country. In 1974, the country became a republic.

After the Second World War, Greece and Turkey disagreed over the island of Cyprus. This independent country is home to both Greeks and Turks. In 1974, Turkey invaded Cyprus. The island is divided and the United Nation keep the peace between the Greeks and Turks there.

Modern Greece

In the last 70 years, Greece has had many different types of government. Greek people are talking about how to protect the environment and about Greece's place in the European Union. The country still has problems, but it is looking forward to the future.

▼ Greek school girls

Fact file

Government

Greece is a democratic republic. It is a member of the European Union. All Greeks over 18 years old vote for their government.

The Greek Parliament is the *Vouli*. It has 300 members, or deputies, who serve for four years. The Prime Minister is the leader of the party with the largest number of deputies in the *Vouli*. The *Vouli* elects a head of state, the President, who serves for five years.

Flag and anthem

The Greek flag is striped blue and white. The white cross in the top left corner stands for the Greek Orthodox Church.

The anthem is called the 'Hymn to Freedom'.

Money

The Greek *drachma* is made up of 100 *lepra*.

Peoples and religions

Most people follow the Greek Orthodox Church. There are some Turkish Moslems, some Jewish people, and Albanian, Slav, Gypsy and Vlach peoples.

Education

Children must go to school from the age of six until they are 15. Education is free, but there are fee-paying schools as well. There are nursery schools, primary and secondary schools, colleges and universities.

Festivals and holidays

Easter is the most important Christian religious festival. Independence Day is 25 March, and May Day is 1 May.

Newspapers, TV, radio

There are two government TV channels, ET1 and ET2, as well as cable and satellite TV. There are many different Greek radio stations and newspapers.

Some famous people

Homer (c850-800BCE) wrote long poems about Greek heroes.

Sappho (c650BCE) was the greatest woman poet of the ancient world.

Hippocrates (c460-377 or 359 BCE) was a doctor, called 'the father of medicine' today.

Plato (c428-348BCE) wrote the *Republic*, about government.

Alexander the Great (356-323BCE) was a great military leader and an emperor.

Theodora (c500-548) was an empress of Byzantium.

Domenico Theotocopoulos (1541-1614) was a Cretan painter. He was called 'El Greco', 'the Greek'.

Andreas Papandreou (1919-96) became the first socialist Prime Minister in 1981.

Melina Mercouri (1925-1994) was a film actress who became a government minister.

Some key events in history

c2000BCE (Before Christian Era) The Minoans built Knossós.

508: Democracy in Athens.

338: Macedonia ruled Greece.

146: Rome ruled Greece.

330CE (Christian Era): Byzantium became capital of the eastern Roman empire.

1453: Constantinople fell.

1830: Greece became an independent nation.

1917-18: Greece entered the First World War.

1941-44: Germany occupied Greece in Second World War.

1944-49: Civil War in Greece.

1949: Monarchy in Greece.

1967-74: Military rule.

1974: Greece became a democratic republic.

1981: Greece joined the European Union.

1996: Violence between Greeks and Turks on Cyprus.

Index